John Williams
Anthology

VOLONTÈ&Co

Foto di copertina:
© 2010 Matthew Cavanaugh
www.matthewcavanaugh.com

INDEX

CADILLAC OF THE SKIES
(from Empire of the Sun)

Music by John Williams

CAN YOU READ MY MIND

(Love Theme from Superman)

Lyrics by Leslie Bricusse - Music by John Williams

DOUBLE TROUBLE
(from Harry Potter and The Prisoner of Azkaban)

Words and Music by John Williams

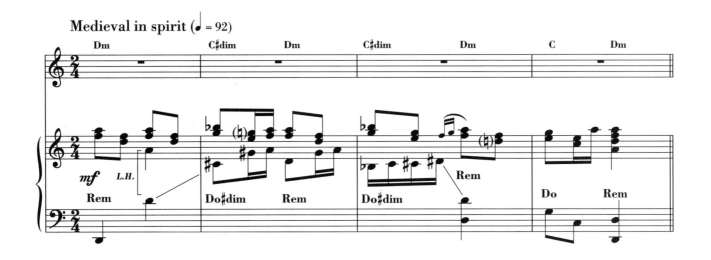

Driving now, with a "swagger"

HEDWIG'S THEME
(from Harry Potter and the Sorcerer's Stone)

Music by John Williams

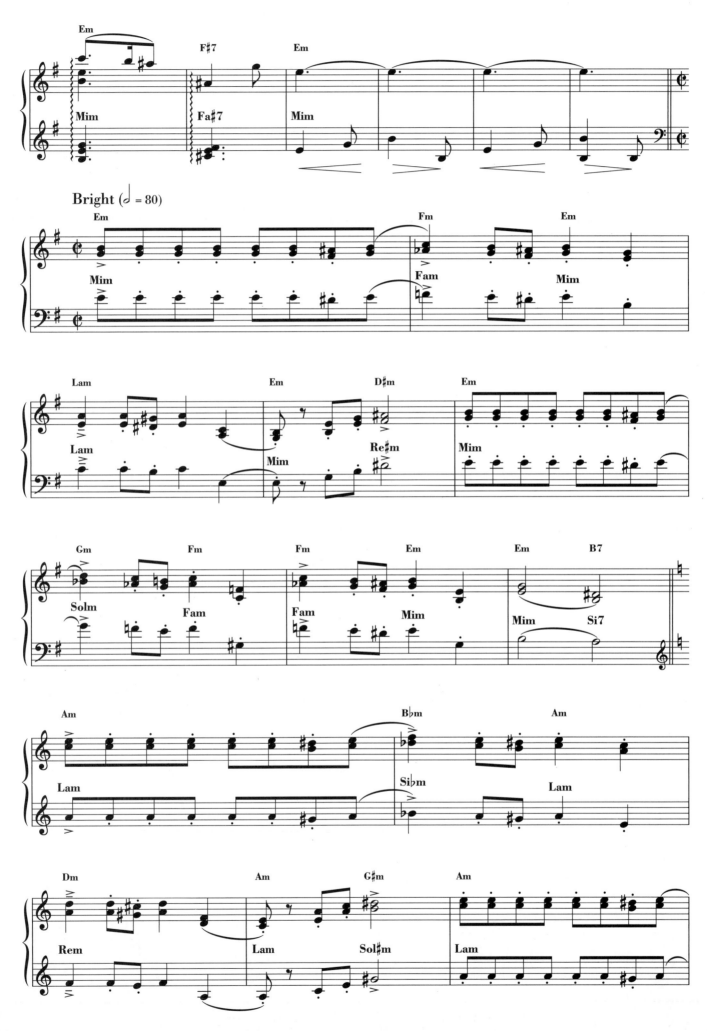

FLIGHT TO NEVERLAND
(from Hook)

Music by John Williams

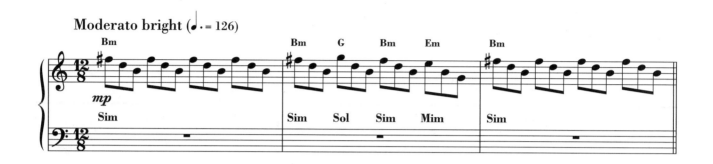

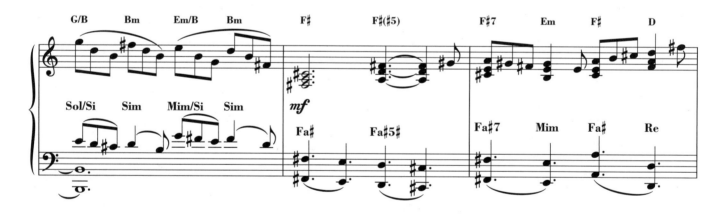

HARRY'S WONDROUS WORLD

(from Harry Potter and the Sorcerer's Stone)

Music by John Williams

Stately and nobly

PARADE OF THE SLAVE CHILDREN
(from Indiana Jones And The Temple Of Doom)

Words and Music by John Williams

THE RAIDERS MARCH
(from Raiders Of The Lost Ark a/k/a Indiana Jones Theme)

Music by John Williams

STAR WARS
(Main Theme)

Music by John Williams

THE IMPERIAL MARCH

(Darth Vader's Theme from Star Wars: Episode V The Empire Strikes Back)

Music by John Williams

THEME FROM SCHINDLER'S LIST

(from Schindler's List)

Music by John Williams

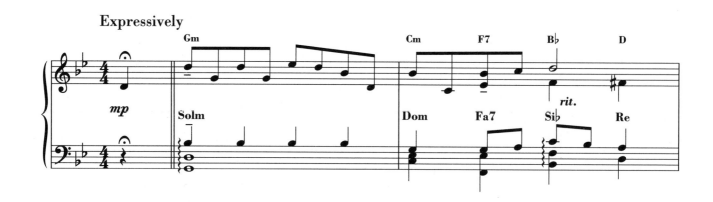

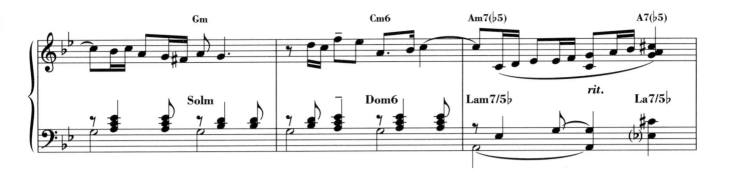

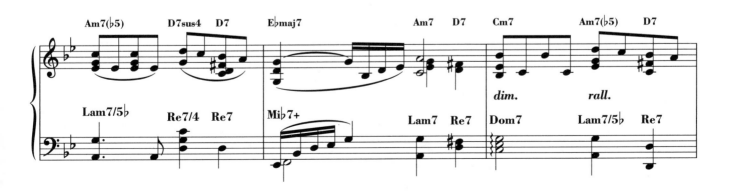

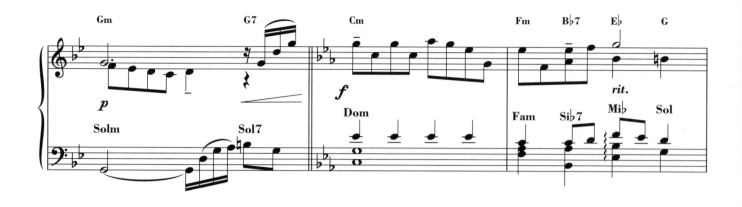

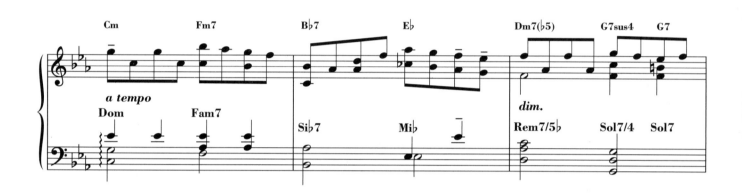

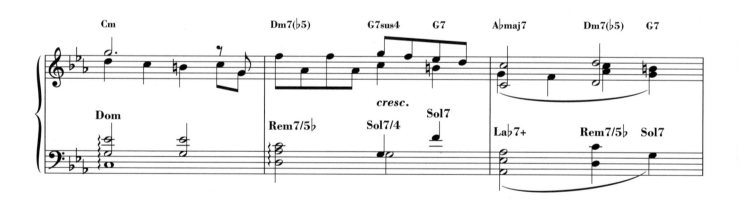

THEME FROM SUPERMAN
(from Superman)

Music by John Williams

Stampa: Geca Industrie Grafiche • San Giuliano Milanese (Mi) • Maggio 2015
Printed in Italy